PRESENTED TO

WITH LOVE FROM

DATE

Lord, teach a little child to pray,
And then accept my prayer,
Thou hearest all the words I say
For Thou art everywhere.

JANE TAYLOR

Published in Nashville, Tennessee, by Tommy Nelson®,
a division of Thomas Nelson, Inc.

Unless otherwise indicated, Scripture quotations are from the
International Children's Bible®, *New Century Version*®, copyright © 1986, 1988, 1999
by Tommy Nelson®, a division of Thomas Nelson, Inc. Used by permission.

ISBN 0-8499-7767-3

Library of Congress Control Number: 2001132128

Printed in China

01 02 03 04 05 LEO 5 4 3 2 1

THOMAS KINKADE

Bedtime Prayers

NELSON

Thomas Nelson, Inc.
Nashville

I can lie down and go to sleep.
And I will wake up again because the Lord protects me.

PSALM 3:5

Now I lay me down to sleep.
I pray You, Lord, my soul to keep.
Your love be with me through the night
And wake me with the morning light.

TRADITIONAL

Lord, You made the stars that brightly
Twinkle in the nighttime sky.
You made the clouds that float lightly
Above the trees and mountains high.
Lord, You know each one by number.
Your watchful eyes never slumber.
O Lord who made the stars above,
Watch me, guard me with Your love.

UNKNOWN

Lord, keep me safe this night,
Secure from all my fears;
May angels guard me while I sleep,
Till morning light appears.

JOHN LELAND (Adapted)

O, holy Father, I thank You
for all the blessings of this day.
Forgive me for that which I have done wrong.
Bless me and keep me through the night,
For Jesus' sake.
Amen.

UNKNOWN

Father, we thank you for the night,
And for the pleasant morning light;
For rest and food and loving care,
And all that makes the day so fair.

Help us to do the things we should,
To be to others kind and good;
In all we do at work or play
To grow more loving every day.

REBECCA J. WESTON

All night, all day,
Angels watching over me, my Lord.
All night, all day,
Angels watching over me.
Sun is a-setting in the West;
Angels watching over me, my Lord.
Sleep my child, take your rest;
Angels watching over me.
All night, all day,
Angels watching over me, my Lord.
All night, all day,
Angels watching over me.

UNKNOWN

Loving Shepherd of your sheep
Keep your lamb in safety, keep;
Nothing can your power withstand,
None can pluck me from your hand.

JANE ELIZA LEESON

Our Father in heaven,

we pray that your name

will always be kept holy.

We pray that your kingdom will come.

We pray that what you want will be done,

here on earth as it is in heaven.

Give us the food we need for each day.

Forgive the sins we have done,

just as we have forgiven those

who did wrong to us.

Do not cause us to be tested;

but save us from the Evil One.

MATTHEW 6:9–13

Through the night your angels kept
Watch beside me while I slept;
Now the dark has gone away;
Thank you, Lord, for this new day.

WILLIAM CANTON (Adapted)

Jesus, tender Shepherd, hear me,
Bless your little lamb tonight;
Through the darkness please be near me,
Keep me safe till morning light.

All this day your hand has led me,
And I thank you for your care;
You have clothed me, warmed and fed me,
Listen to my evening prayer.

Let my sins be all forgiven;
Bless the friends I love so well;
Take me, when I die to heaven,
Happy there with you to dwell.

MARY L. DUNCAN

Now the day is over,
Night is drawing nigh,
Shadows of the evening
Steal across the sky.

Now the darkness gathers,
Stars begin to peep,
Birds and beasts and flowers
Soon will be asleep.

Jesus, give the weary
Calm and sweet repose;
With your tender blessings
May our eyelids close.

Through the long night watches,
May your angels spread
Their white wings above me,
Watching round my bed.

When the morning wakens,
Then may I arise
Pure, and fresh, and sinless
In your holy eyes.

SABINE BARING-GOULD (Adapted)

Angels at the foot,
And Angels at the head,
And like a curly little lamb
My pretty babe in bed.

CHRISTINA ROSSETTI

My Father, for another night
Of quiet sleep and rest,
For all the joy of morning light,
Your holy name be blessed.

HENRY WILLIAM BAKER (Adapted)

This little light of mine,
I'm gonna let it shine.
This little light of mine,
I'm gonna let it shine.
This little light of mine,
I'm gonna let it shine.
Let it shine,
Let it shine,
Let it shine.

UNKNOWN

Savior, teach me, day by day,
Love's sweet lesson to obey;
Sweeter lesson cannot be,
Loving Him who first loved me.

JANE ELIZA LEESON

Gentle Jesus, meek and mild,
Look upon a little child;

Lamb of God, I look to Thee;
You shall my example be;

You are gentle, meek and mild,
You were once a little child.

Let me above all fulfill
God my heavenly Father's will;

Loving Jesus, gentle Lamb,
In Your gracious hands I am,

Make me, Savior, what You are,
Live Yourself within my heart.

CHARLES WESLEY
"Lamb of God I Look to Thee"

I look at the heavens,
which you made with your hands.
I see the moon and stars,
which you created.

PSALM 8:3

O God,
You spoke and the sky appeared.
You breathed and stars filled the sky.
You made the oceans and the seas,
and you filled all the earth with your love.
Thank you, God, for this wonderful world. Amen.

[Based on Psalm 33:5–9]

TAMA FORTNER

I see the moon,
And the moon sees me;
God bless the moon,
And God bless me.

OLD NURSERY RHYME

He counts the stars and names each one.

PSALM 147:4

Star light, star bright,
First star I see tonight,
I wish I may, I wish I might,
Have the wish I wish tonight.

MOTHER GOOSE

God made the sun
  And God made the tree,
God made the mountains
  And God made me.

I thank you, O God,
  For the sun and the tree,
For making the mountains
  And for making me.

LEAH GALE

"A Birthday Grace"

You made my whole being. You formed me in my mother's body.
I praise you because you made me in an amazing and wonderful way
What you have done is wonderful. I know this very well.

PSALM 139:13–14

God made the world so broad and grand,
Filled with blessings from His hand.
He made the sky so high and blue,
And all the little children too!

UNKNOWN

Obey the Lord your God.
Then all these blessings will come and stay with you.

DEUTERONOMY 28:2

Thanks to you, kind Father
For my daily bread,
For my home and playthings,
For my cozy bed.

Mother, father, dear ones—
Bless them while I pray:
May I try to help them,
Cheerfully obey.

CHARLES HEALING

All good gifts around us
Are sent from heaven above;
Then thank the Lord,
    O thank the Lord,
For all his love.

MATTHIAS CLAUDIUS

The Lord is good to me,
    and so I thank the Lord.
For giving me the things I need:
    the sun, the rain, and the apple seed!
The Lord is good to me.

TRADITIONAL

Lord, teach a little child to pray,
    And then accept my prayer,
You hear all the words I say
    For You are everywhere.

A little sparrow cannot fall
    Unnoticed, Lord, by Thee;
And though I am so young and small
    You take good care of me.

Teach me to do the thing that's right,
    And when I sin, forgive;
And make it still my chief delight
    To serve You while I live.

JANE TAYLOR (Adapted)

"Lord, please teach us how to pray."

LUKE 11:1

Index of Paintings